The 1940s

From World War II to Jackie Robinson

Stephen Feinstein

Enslow Publishers, Inc.

40 Industrial Road   PO Box 38
Box 398   Aldershot
Berkeley Heights, NJ 07922   Hants GU12 6BP
USA   UK

http://www.enslow.com

Library of Congress Cataloging-in-Publication Data

Feinstein, Stephen.
    The 1940s from World War II to Jackie Robinson / Stephen Feinstein.
        p. cm. — (Decades of the 20th century)
    Includes index.
    Summary: Discusses the fashions, fads, politics, advances in medicine and technology, people, and world issues that made the 1940s a unique time in American and world history.
    ISBN 0-7660-1428-2
    1. United States—Civilization—1918–1945—Juvenile literature. 2. United States—Civilization—1945– —Juvenile literature. 3. Nineteen forties—Juvenile literature. 4. World War, 1939–1945—Juvenile literature. [1. United States—Civilization. 2. Nineteen forties. 3. World War, 1939–1945.]
    I. Title. II. Decades of the twentieth century.
    E169.12 .F446 2000
    973.9—dc21
                                                        99-050710

Printed in the United States of America

10 9 8 7 6 5 4 3 2

To Our Readers:
We have done our best to make sure all Internet addresses in this book were active and appropriate when we went to press. However, the author and the publisher have no control over and assume no liability for the material available on those Internet sites or on other Web sites they may link to. Any comments or suggestions can be sent by e-mail to comments@enslow.com or to the address on the back cover.

Illustration Credits: Archive Photos, p. 23; Bert Randolph Sugar, *The Great Baseball Players from McGraw to Mantle* (Mineola, N.Y.: Dover Publications, Inc., 1977), pp. 3, 26, 27, 28, 61B; Courtesy of Henrietta Oppenheim, p. 10; Enslow Publishers, Inc., p. 55; Frank Driggs/Archive Photos, p. 11; Library of Congress, pp. 3, 4, 12, 13, 18, 22, 24, 25, 30, 37, 38, 43, 51, 52, 61; *Movie Star Postcards* (Dover Publications, Inc., 1986), pp. 1, 17, 60; National Archives, pp. 1, 2, 5, 6, 7, 8, 9, 14, 16–17, 20, 29, 31, 33, 34, 35, 36, 39, 40, 41, 42, 44, 45, 46, 47, 48, 53, 56, 57, 58, 59, 60, 61; Photofest, pp. 20, 21; Reproduced from the *Dictionary of American Portraits*, Published by Dover Publications, Inc., in 1967, p. 19; Unisys Corporation, p. 54.

Cover Illustrations: Bert Randolph Sugar, *The Great Baseball Players from McGraw to Mantle* (Mineola, N.Y.: Dover Publications, Inc., 1977); Library of Congress; National Archives.

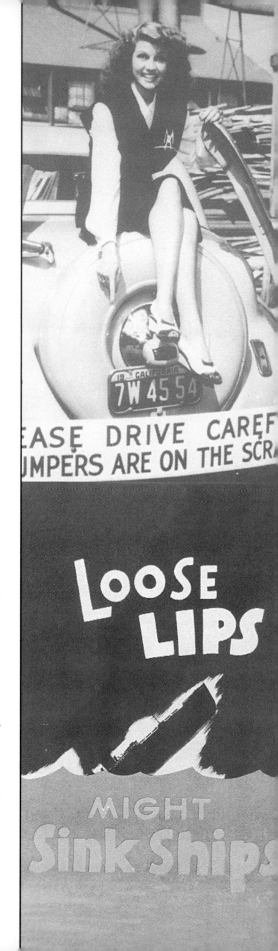

Contents

The 1930s were difficult years for most Americans. Millions had to endure extreme poverty and hunger during the Great Depression, an economic collapse that affected the whole world. Under President Franklin D. Roosevelt, the nation pulled out of the depths of the Depression. But the economy was still weak, and many Americans were still unemployed.

As the 1940s began, Americans hoped for an improvement in their lives—better job opportunities and financial security. Although much of the world was at war, Americans were more concerned with domestic matters. In fact, most thought isolationism—avoiding involvement in conflicts abroad—was the best policy for America. As bad as things seemed overseas, the problems there did not seem to concern America. When Roosevelt ran for an unprecedented third term as president in 1940, he told Americans that he would not send their sons to fight overseas. This was what Americans wanted to hear. They voted Roosevelt into office again.

On December 7, 1941, Japan carried out a surprise air attack on the United States naval base at Pearl Harbor, Hawaii. By December 11, the United States was at war. By its end in 1945, the war would change the United States, its economy, and the decade of the 1940s in dramatic ways.

In this famous photograph by Dorothea Lange (opposite) from the Great Depression, a migrant farmworker woman tries to comfort her two children. During the Depression, many businesses closed, leaving thousands of Americans without jobs, and forcing many families to suffer terrible poverty.

The day after the Japanese attack on the United States naval base at Pearl Harbor, Hawaii (below), President Roosevelt, referring to December 7 as "a date which will live in infamy," responded by asking Congress to declare war on Japan.

I WANT YOU

for the **U.S. ARMY**
ENLIST NOW

Wartime Rationing and Victory Gardens

Americans were used to buying whatever they wanted whenever they wanted— if they had enough money to make the purchase. Once the United States entered World War II, people were suddenly faced with restrictions on what and how much they could buy.

On December 27, 1941, the government announced a rationing of rubber tires. A rubber shortage had come about almost overnight. Soon the new federal Office of Price Administration (OPA) announced that various other goods would also be strictly rationed, including sugar, coffee, meat, fats and oils, cheese, and shoes. The OPA also issued books of ration stamps, which had to be used to buy rationed goods.

Americans had no choice but to go along with the OPA's rationing system. Surprisingly, Americans ate better during the war years than they did during the 1930s. Even though many food products were strictly rationed, the need for factories to produce huge amounts of goods for fighting the war meant that most people had jobs. They could afford to buy more of whatever was available.

Another factor contributed to the nation's food supply during the war. The government encouraged Americans to plant vegetables in their backyards. That way, commercial farmers could feed the army rather than ordinary customers. Inspired by feelings of patriotism and a sense of practicality, many Americans enthusiastically

Posters like this one (opposite) called upon Americans to do their duty by committing to fight the war. World War II would affect all aspects of American life, not only for those who responded to recruitment advertisements and joined the armed services, but for those left on the home front.

Americans were encouraged to grow their own food in "Victory Gardens" (above), to allow commercial farmers to devote their efforts to helping the armed forces fight the war.

grew "Victory Gardens," as their backyard minifarms were called. In 1943, Victory Gardens produced about one third of all the vegetables consumed in the United States.

Rosie the Riveter

During the war years, the number of American women who worked increased from about 12 million to about 18.5 million. Inspired by Lockheed Aircraft's mythical Rosie the Riveter, whose picture appeared on posters all around the country, many women put on coveralls and followed Rosie to jobs at defense-related factories. Women soon proved just as good as men at performing many of the industrial assembly-line jobs that had been previously held only by men.

By the end of the war, women made up about 36 percent of the civilian workforce. With their help, wartime production had proceeded at an astounding pace. The sheer volume of American production was overwhelming. It helped bring the United States and its allies victory in the war. In just five years, 1940–1945, United States factories produced almost three hundred thousand aircraft, seventy-one thousand naval ships, five thousand cargo ships, about three hundred thousand artillery pieces, 20 million small arms, 41.5 billion rounds of small arms ammunition, almost 6 million aircraft bombs, more

Because so many men were overseas fighting the war, women had to step in to fill jobs formerly held only by men. Rosie the Riveter (below) became one of the most famous images of the female workforce during World War II.

We Can Do It!

WAR PRODUCTION CO-ORDINATING COMMITTEE

than one hundred thousand tanks and self-propelled guns, and about 2.5 million army trucks.

WACs, WAVES, and WAFS

Not only were American women working at factory jobs, but for the first time, some women enlisted in the military. Some served in the new Women's Army Auxiliary Corps (WACs). Others joined a branch of the navy called Women Accepted for Volunteer Emergency Service (WAVES). And some women served as fliers in the Women's Auxiliary Ferrying Squadron (WAFS). Women were not assigned to combat duty. Instead, they did jobs that allowed more men to be available for combat. By 1945, more than two hundred thousand women were actively serving in the armed forces.

Women took all kinds of jobs to help the war effort on the home front. These women (below) worked at repairing railroad tracks. Companies encouraged women workers. "If you can drive a car, you can run a machine," was the slogan of one military supply company in Connecticut that campaigned to hire an additional five thousand women.

Shortages caused by the war brought changes in fashion. Both men and women (above) wore simple, tailored garments that required less fabric than the styles of earlier years. Women, however, still showed their femininity with slim waistlines and full skirts.

Clothes for War, Clothes for Peace

Because much of the nation's clothing industry during the war was working to provide uniforms for the military, there was far less fabric for other kinds of clothing. The government set strict guidelines on the amount of fabric to be used in various items of clothing. Fabric shortages encouraged a trend toward simpler styles, such as wraparound skirts.

Long evening dresses were replaced with shorter ones. Short sleeves replaced long sleeves. Coats had no cuffs, and blouses had no pockets or ruffles. Because there were also restrictions on the use of metal for zippers and other fasteners, designers created a dress that draped so that it needed only two buttons. Women who worked in factories wore the same type of clothing on the job as their male coworkers. Work outfits were sturdy coveralls or jumpsuits, hard hats, tool belts, and thick-soled shoes. Away from the job, women preferred clothing that showed their femininity, such as belted or tailored dresses that were pinched in the waist.

After the war, women's fashion took off in a completely different direction. No longer were fabrics in short supply. Paris, which had been occupied by Germany during the war, was once again the center of fashion. Parisian fashion designer Christian Dior introduced his "New Look," which emphasized a woman's curves. His designs featured a tiny waistline; long, full skirts; sloping shoulders; and soft, full collars and sleeves.

Better Than Silk

In 1940, Du Pont introduced a new synthetic fiber called nylon. It was said to be as strong as elastic, but it had the sheerness of silk. The company planned to use nylon to replace the traditional silk stocking.

Once America entered the war, silk stockings became unavailable because Japan, one of the nations that the United States was fighting, stopped exporting silk. As a result, the United States government ordered that all nylon be used to make parachutes, tents, and other war supplies—not women's stockings. During the war, some women drew fake seams on their legs with an eyebrow pencil to make it look as though they were wearing stockings, even though they were not.

Zoot suits, worn mainly by young men, were partly responsible for one of Los Angeles, California's most notorious riots. Below, popular band leader Cab Calloway shows off the zoot suit look.

Zoot Suits

Young men, mainly African Americans and poor whites, began wearing a new type of out-fit in the early 1940s that defied conventional styles. Known as a zoot suit, the style featured baggy pants that tapered from sixteen inches wide at the knee to six inches at the pegged bottom. With the pants was a jacket with over-stuffed shoulders that reached down to the knees and was usually worn unbuttoned. A key chain that almost dragged on the floor was often worn.

The baggy zoot suit fad also became very popular with young Mexican Americans, known as Pachucos, in Los Angeles, California. Unfortunately, the zoot suit played a key role

11

World War II increased production in almost every American industry, which brought the nation out of the depths of the Great Depression and eventually began a new era of prosperity. The huge demand for industrial products during wartime can be seen in this busy tractor plant (above).

The skimpy woman's swimsuit called the bikini was named for this island, Bikini Atoll (opposite), where the United States tested nuclear weapons in the years after World War II. The native people of Bikini, however, profited little from the publicity. Most were forced to relocate, and the island was devastated by nuclear fallout.

in a shameful episode of racist violence. In June 1943, in Los Angeles, a mob of about twenty-five hundred white sailors and soldiers attacked about one hundred Mexican Americans wearing zoot suits. Supposedly, there had been a rumor that a gang of Pachucos had beaten up a sailor. In response, the servicemen began beating up anyone they saw wearing a zoot suit. After the military police put an end to the riot, the Los Angeles City Council outlawed the wearing of zoot suits.

The Baby Boom

In the early 1940s, the birthrate began to rise dramatically. Many young couples rushed to get married and have children before the husband could be sent off to war. By 1943, the birthrate had risen to a sixteen-year peak.

But it was not until after the war, in 1946, that the true baby boom, which would last for the next eighteen years, began. The war was over. The husbands were back. And young men and women who were still single rushed to get married. It was a perfect time to start a family. Jobs were plentiful, rationing had ended, and America seemed prosperous. In 1946, the birthrate had increased by about 20 percent from the previous year.

12

Seventy-four percent of couples had their first child during their first year of marriage.

The Bomb and the Bikini

In 1946, a new type of swimwear, called a bikini, was introduced. It was named after Bikini Atoll, a small island in the western Pacific Ocean. On Bikini, the United States had tested nuclear bombs. For most Americans, who were used to one-piece bathing suits, the sight of a woman on the beach in a skimpy two-piece bathing suit was quite startling. It would take years for the novelty to wear off and for the racy new swimsuit to become a common sight.

Postwar Prosperity

The major social and cultural trends that would characterize the 1950s began during the years immediately following the end of World War II. While the majority of Americans before the war were poor, most Americans after the war had money to spend. A vast new middle class of consumers bought new cars, new homes in new suburban subdivisions, and all kinds of household appliances, including a revolutionary new appliance called a television.

BUY WAR BONDS

The War as Entertainment

The arts and entertainment in America during the war years could not avoid being influenced by World War II. Popular songs of the times included tunes such as "Let's Knock the Hit out of Hitler," "He's 1-A in the Army and He's A-1 in My Heart," and "The Boogie Woogie Bugle Boy of Company B."

Popular comic strip heroes such as Ham Fisher's boxer Joe Palooka joined the army for the duration of the war. Curiously, Superman was ruled 4-F, or ineligible for service, by his local draft board because of his X-ray vision! Instead of fighting America's enemies, the man of steel had to spend the war years raising money for the Red Cross. Meanwhile, Little Orphan Annie went around urging kids to collect scrap metal for the war effort.

Likewise, illustrator Norman Rockwell created a series of *Saturday Evening Post* covers featuring Willie Gillis, a young man who goes off to war and finally returns home safely. One of Rockwell's covers also featured Rosie the Riveter.

Hollywood Responds to the War

Movies probably did the most to evoke feelings of patriotism and raise people's spirits. Hollywood cranked out an endless stream of war-related movies throughout the war years. Even during the period before America's entry into the war, Hollywood had begun to release films with an anti-Nazi message. (Nazis were the Germans under Adolf Hitler against whom the Allies were

World War II affected not only the soldiers who were fighting and their loved ones at home, but even the entertainment industry. The messages of posters like this one (opposite), encouraging Americans to buy war bonds, were echoed by many famous Hollywood movie stars, who also worked at selling war bonds in support of the war effort.

fighting in Europe.) Among these films were *Confessions of a Nazi Spy* (1939); *The Great Dictator* (1940), Charlie Chaplin's spoof of Hitler; and *I Married a Nazi* (1940).

Within six months of the bombing of Pearl Harbor, seventy war-related movies were released in theaters. Many were about real events, such as *Remember Pearl Harbor*. Because of America's anger toward Japan, these films often used terrible racist stereotyping, depicting the Japanese as evil, bucktoothed, subhuman caricatures.

Other films were about typical Hollywood heroes, such as Tarzan, who now had to fight Nazis in the African jungle.

After Nazi Germany invaded Poland in September 1939 (opposite and left), the American film industry responded to the threat of Nazism in Europe by releasing many war films and other movies that criticized the Germans.

Famous Hollywood stars, such as Lauren Bacall and Humphrey Bogart (above), appeared in films that indirectly supported the United States war effort.

There were also gangster movies in which the "bad guys" became Nazi spies. Various other Hollywood movies portrayed the contributions and sacrifices of Americans who played important roles in the war effort. Possibly the biggest hit film of the World War II years was *Casablanca* (1942), starring Humphrey Bogart and Ingrid Bergman. In addition to popular films, directors such as Frank Capra produced a series of documentaries called *Why We Fight*. They explained how the United States had become involved in the war. Even

Walt Disney created films in support of the war effort, such as *Victory Through Airpower*.

To make sure that Hollywood filmmakers were giving the appropriate message, in June 1942, President Roosevelt created the Office of War Information (OWI), a government propaganda agency. The OWI set up an office in Hollywood. Studios were asked to submit film scripts before shooting began. The OWI reviewed scripts and suggested changes, if necessary, so that the film would present the government's view of the country and the war.

Hollywood During the Cold War

Under the supervision and enthusiastic support of the OWI, Hollywood produced a number of propaganda films, including *The North Star* (1943), which portrayed America's Soviet allies in a sympathetic light. *The North Star*'s screenplay was written by Lillian Hellman, its musical score was by Aaron Copland, and its lyrics were by Ira Gershwin.

But in the years after the war, the political landscape of the world changed radically. The Soviet Union, America's wartime ally, had become the United States' enemy. After World War II ended, the victorious Allies divided Europe among themselves to ensure that the war-torn countries would be rebuilt and governed properly. The Communist Soviet Union took over the governments of

After the war ended, America and the Soviet Union began to regard each other as a threat. Before long, relations between the two nations became so strained that a "Cold War" began. It was a state of hostility that would divide much of the world into two main camps: the Free World—America and its Western allies, and the Communist World—the Soviet Union and its Eastern European satellites and China. Propaganda posters (below) depicted the Soviets as a menacing presence.

SIBERIE

several Eastern European nations and made them part of the Communist system. The United States feared communism, believing its goal was to take over the whole world and eliminate democratic systems such as America's. Therefore, many American leaders worked hard to prevent Soviet influence from spreading. During the long period known as the Cold War, the United States and the Soviet Union opposed each other fiercely, each building weapons and trying to gain influence with other nations around the world. However, the two nations never fought an actual battle.

Cold War tensions carried over into many aspects of American life. Although President Harry Truman disbanded the OWI in 1945, Hollywood's brief period of freedom from government interference came to an end in 1947. That year, the newly established House Committee on Un-American Activities (HUAC) began investigating Hollywood. Committee members looked for Communists working in the film industry—people "guilty" of producing pro-Soviet films such as *Song of Russia* and *The North Star*.

In October 1947, HUAC held hearings in Washington, D.C. Among those summoned to testify were ten Hollywood screenwriters. A group of Hollywood celebrities, including Humphrey Bogart, Lauren Bacall, John Huston, and Danny Kaye, traveled to Washington to protest the hearings. The "Hollywood Ten," as the screenwriters were called, refused to cooperate with the committee. They were fined and jailed. They were among hundreds who would be blacklisted. (A blacklist held names of people that the makers of the list considered dangerous or unacceptable.) No studio would hire them for many years to come.

President Harry S Truman, who led the United States through the early years of Cold War tensions with the Soviet Union, is perhaps best remembered as the man who made the controversial decision to drop the atomic bomb on Japan to end World War II. Even years later, Truman defended his decision, saying the use of the atomic bomb saved the lives of thousands of American soldiers.

HUAC hearings against suspected Communists in the film industry caused outrage among many famous American actors. Seen above entertaining soldiers during World War II, film and stage star Danny Kaye was one of many celebrities who strongly protested the "Hollywood Ten" hearings.

Film noir was considered strange by many American filmgoers when it first appeared. But Americans came to accept and enjoy the dark style of the films, especially those that starred popular actors such as Humphrey Bogart (right).

Film Noir

After the war ended, a new type of suspense film known as film noir became popular in the United States. Movies of this genre, filmed in stark black and white and featuring odd camera angles, usually had a bleak urban setting. Their stories were often based on detective novels. The hero typically had to deal with personal obsessions, dangerous delusions, and romantic or other goals that were difficult or impossible to achieve. It seems strange that a dark, moody type of film could have struck a chord with American movie-goers in a time of optimism and prosperity. Perhaps the growing sense of insecurity that came with the onset of the Cold War had something to do with it. Or perhaps the horrors of World War II had given Americans a cynical awareness and appreciation of the dark side of human nature.

The first noir film was director John Huston's *The Maltese Falcon*, starring Humphrey Bogart. Produced in 1941, it would influence the film noir movies made after the war.

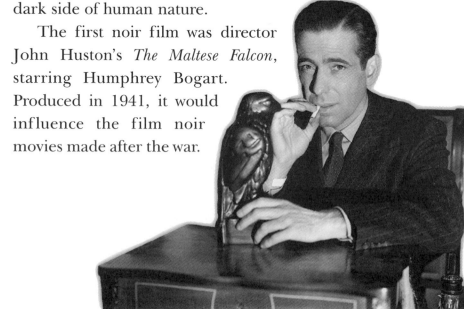

The Greatest Film That Hardly Anyone Saw: Citizen Kane

Orson Welles's *Citizen Kane* (1943) is often considered "the greatest film ever made." Yet very few people in the 1940s ever had the opportunity to see it.

Welles created a devastating fictional portrayal of the life of powerful newspaper publisher William Randolph Hearst. RKO Studios had allowed twenty-five-year-old Welles to produce the film without any supervision or interference from studio executives. When Hearst learned about the film, however, he tried to prevent its release by threatening legal action against RKO. As a result, there was only a limited release of *Citizen Kane*. Still, critics loved it, and the movie won nine Academy Award nominations and one Oscar for best screenplay.

Winning fame as both a screen star and director, Orson Welles (below) was often a controversial figure in the entertainment industry. In 1938, he terrified radio listeners with his Halloween production of H. G. Wells's War of the Worlds. Many listeners, who missed the portion of the radio program that identified it as a fictional drama, actually believed the story—that Martians had landed in New Jersey!

Modernism in Fiction

Many American novelists during the 1940s also focused on the war. Thus, a new type of fiction was born, known as the combat novel. The best of this genre included works such as Norman Mailer's *The Naked and the Dead* (1948).

Writers in the 1940s focused on the individual and his or her place in the modern world. Representing this new style of "modernism" in American writing were novelists such as Saul Bellow, Truman Capote, Paul Bowles, and John Hawkes.

African-American writer Richard Wright was also popular. He dealt with the oppression of blacks, but his work was closer in spirit to the Socialist realist writers of the 1930s. His novel *Native Son* (1940) and autobiography, *Black Boy* (1945), were widely read by white Americans as well as blacks.

Richard Wright (below) became known as one of the most outspoken critics of racial discrimination in the United States. Even in the 1940s, African Americans were subject to Jim Crow, or segregation, laws, especially in the South. Wright's work showed the injustice and violence African Americans faced on a daily basis.

Realism in the Theater

The two most successful American playwrights of the 1940s were Tennessee Williams and Arthur Miller. Both men tried to depict life in America realistically. Thomas Lanier Williams, who became known as Tennessee Williams, focused on the frustrations, illusions, and emotional conflicts of ordinary people in his plays *The Glass Menagerie* (1945), *A Streetcar Named Desire* (1947), and *Summer and Smoke* (1948). Arthur Miller, in his plays *All My Sons* (1947) and *Death of a Salesman* (1949), dealt with the conflict between fathers and sons.

Fantasy in the Theater

Throughout the 1940s, the Broadway musical proved to be popular with many Americans. Audiences probably enjoyed a couple of hours of escape from the world's troubles just as much as they appreciated the musicals' spectacular dancing and memorable tunes. Especially successful were Rodgers and Hammerstein's *Oklahoma!* (1943) and *Carousel* (1945), Irving Berlin's *Annie Get Your Gun* (1946), and Cole Porter's *Kiss Me, Kate* (1948).

"Mr. Television"

A major innovation that would have an effect on the lifestyles of Americans and people all over the world had been in development for years. On July 1, 1941, the CBS and NBC television networks began broadcasting fifteen hours of programming a week. But television sets were very expensive. By late 1941, only about fifteen thousand televisions were in use. Once the United States entered World War II, further development of television was put on hold. After the war, television production and broadcasting resumed. Television sets soon became much more affordable.

The most popular show in the late 1940s was *Texaco Star Theater*. It was a variety show starring comedian Milton Berle. By the fall of 1948, 94.7 percent of television viewers in the United States were watching *Texaco Star Theater*. Berle became known as Mr. Television. Many American television viewers affectionately referred to him as "Uncle Miltie."

Children were also captivated by television. Shows such as *Howdy Doody* attracted a devoted audience of baby boomers.

Despite limited programming, television swept the United States in the 1940s. Especially after World War II, when Americans were enjoying postwar prosperity, televisions became affordable to many households. Over the years, the new entertainment medium would come to replace the radio, which had been the focal point of most American living rooms for decades.

The Crooner and the Bobby-soxers

Teenage girls in the 1940s who were known as bobby-soxers liked to wear striped football socks along with their baggy, rolled-up

Bobby-soxers loved to hang out at local ice cream shops, which were frequently located inside drugstores. There, one of the most memorable images was the soda jerk (above), as ice cream counter clerks were called, who served snacks and ice cream sodas to the crowds of teenage bobby-soxers.

blue jeans and sloppy shirttails. For laughs, they would often purposely wear mismatched socks and shoes.

A favorite bobby-soxer hangout was the local soda shop. There, they could listen to their favorite songs on the jukebox. They were passionate about dancing the lindy, a form of jitterbug, to the big-band swing music of Glenn Miller, Count Basie, Benny Goodman, and others. But bobby-soxers went absolutely crazy over a blue-eyed young singer with a smooth voice.

Francis Albert "Frank" Sinatra caused screams and squeals of ecstasy from the girls in the audience as soon as he began to croon a romantic ballad. Some bobby-soxers had to be carried away on stretchers. On October 12, 1944, Sinatra was performing at the Paramount Theater in New York City. While the concert was going on, about thirty thousand bobby-soxers were rioting outside the theater in Times Square. Hundreds of riot police officers were rushed in to calm the crowd.

The Birth of Bebop

Big-band swing music, the danceable jazz of the 1930s, maintained its popularity during the 1940s. But later in the decade, young people were drawn to rhythm and blues, a style of music that would evolve into rock 'n' roll in the 1950s. With a few exceptions, such as the Duke Ellington Orchestra, the popularity of swing bands began to decline. Duke Ellington, one of America's greatest composers, over the years had basically transformed his swing band into a jazz orchestra that performed his lengthy concert pieces, such as *Black, Brown, and Beige*, in places such as Carnegie Hall.

Other jazz musicians in the 1940s such as Charlie "Bird" Parker, John Birks "Dizzy" Gillespie, Earl "Bud" Powell, and Theolonious Monk were creating a new type of jazz that came to be called "bebop." The new bebop style featured brilliant improvisation built on complex harmonic structures, played at almost impossibly fast tempos. People who wanted to dance had to go elsewhere. Bebop was for people who wanted to *listen* to music. Bebop was typically performed by small groups—trios, quartets, or quintets. Unlike swing, bebop never became music for a mass audience, but it retained an audience of devoted jazz fans for decades to come.

First becoming popular in the mid-1930s, Duke Ellington (below) and his orchestra helped extend the swing era of the 1930s into the 1940s, with their exciting and innovative big-band music. In recent years, big-band music has enjoyed a wave of popularity, and modern musicians try to imitate the jazz sounds of such artists as Ellington.

Breaking the Color Barrier

Major-league baseball was for whites only—until 1947. That was the year that Branch Rickey, the general manager of the Brooklyn Dodgers, decided that the time had come to integrate professional baseball. He hired Jack Roosevelt "Jackie" Robinson to become the first African American to play in the major leagues. At first, Robinson had to put up with abuse and harassment from prejudiced fans and ball players. But Robinson soon proved his worth to the team.

During his first season in 1947, Robinson scored 125 runs. He managed to steal 29 bases that season, more than anyone else in the league. He was named Rookie of the Year in 1947. Robinson was mainly a second baseman, but he also played as an outfielder and as a first and third baseman. In 1949, he was named the National League's Most Valuable Player. That year, he scored 122 runs, batted in 124 runs, had a total of 203 hits, and led the league with a batting average of .342 and 37 stolen bases.

Once Jackie Robinson broke the color barrier in major-league baseball, other African Americans followed in his footsteps. Before the decade was over, Don Newcombe began pitching for the Dodgers. The New York Giants signed Hank Thompson and Monte Irvin. Pitcher Satchel Paige, Larry Doby, and Luke Easter joined the American League's Cleveland Indians.

Jackie Robinson (opposite), who courageously broke the racial barrier in professional baseball, was not only a talented hitter, but also a formidable base runner. After landing on base, Robinson would hesitate before attempting to steal the next base, almost daring the opposing team to try to pick him off.

Satchel Paige (below), who followed Jackie Robinson in desegregating major-league baseball, was a talented pitcher, famous for his so-called "hesitation pitch," which often had batters swinging not at the ball but at the motion of Paige's foot. Paige was also interesting because no one is sure of his exact age. He was rumored to be forty-two when he started playing in the major leagues—an advanced age for a professional baseball player to begin his career.

27

Women's Baseball

Jackie Robinson was not the only one breaking boundaries in the baseball leagues of the 1940s. Women, too, made an impact, despite the fact that women had never played baseball professionally.

After the bombing of Pearl Harbor, men from all walks of life began joining the military to help the United States and the Allies win the war. Some of the most memorable images of the war years are photographs of famous baseball players such as New York Yankee Joe DiMaggio enlisting to serve in the army. With so many men overseas in combat, there were not enough men left to play major-league baseball.

To keep the game going so that people left on the home front could still enjoy America's favorite pastime, chewing gum tycoon and Chicago Cubs owner Philip Wrigley decided to try to replace the departing baseball players with women. Just as women stepped up to take factory jobs left behind by men, women of ages fifteen to twenty-five joined the All-American Girls Professional Baseball League, beginning in 1943.

Although some minor points of the game were changed, such as overhand pitching, the women played just like men did—but they did it wearing short dresses with satin undergarments! The league had its peak year in 1948, when more than nine hundred thousand people came out to watch the ten women's teams play their season. By 1952, the end of the war and the return of men's

Joe DiMaggio, one of the most famous New York Yankees, made headlines when he enlisted in the army after the United States entered World War II. DiMaggio later became even more famous when he married screen star Marilyn Monroe in the 1950s.

baseball caused attendance to dwindle. The league closed down, but it remains memorable for the unique opportunity it gave to women of the time.

Olympics Are Held Again

In February 1948, American Dick Button won the gold medal for men's figure skating, while Sweden took first place in women's figure skating at the Winter Olympic Games held in St. Moritz, Switzerland. In second and third place were Switzerland and the United States. But the figure skating event, or any other event, was not necessarily as interesting as the fact that the Olympic Games were taking place at all. The 1948 Olympics were the first held since 1936. The games had been suspended because of World War II, which had involved a huge number of the world's nations. So the 1948 games were especially exciting for all those involved.

Women took on the roles formerly held only by men not only in professional sports, but in industry as well. These women (above), called "Chippers," are working for the Marinship Corp. These and many other women devoted their time to the war effort, and in doing so, began to create new ideas about the role of women in American society.

Citation Wins the Triple Crown

The racehorse Citation galloped his way to a Triple Crown victory after having won the Kentucky Derby, Preakness Stakes, and in July 1948, the Belmont Stakes. Citation was ridden by jockey Eddie Arcaro, who had been victorious with Citation before. In fact, after the 1948 Triple Crown win, Arcaro could count four Kentucky Derby wins, two Preakness Stakes wins, and four Belmont Stakes wins—all with Citation. Arcaro's prize money—a total of more than $645,000—was a record for a rider with just one horse.

Isolationists vs. Interventionists

President Franklin Delano Roosevelt was elected to his third term in office in 1940. In order to win the election, he had to walk a fine line between isolationists—Americans who wanted the country to stay out of the war in Europe—and interventionists—those who wanted to join the conflict. Some interventionists believed that America had to act to bring peace and stability to Europe and Asia for the sake of trade and commerce. Some were for direct military involvement. Others thought economic measures would be enough. Roosevelt believed that military intervention would be necessary, but America was not yet ready for this step.

Among the interventionists were Jewish Americans and others who feared that Adolf Hitler, the leader of Nazi Germany, was determined to destroy Europe's Jews. Since coming to power, Hitler had passed many laws taking away the rights of German Jews. Now he was

President Franklin Roosevelt (opposite) is famous not only as the man who helped bring the United States out of the Great Depression with his controversial New Deal programs, but as the only president in American history to have been elected to the nation's highest office four times—in 1932, 1936, 1940, and 1944.

The treatment of German Jews caused fear around the world, but until the start of World War II, few nations made serious efforts to help the Jews being persecuted by Adolf Hitler and his Nazi regime. Below, a group of Jews in Warsaw, Poland, is being arrested by occupying German soldiers, before being sent to concentration camps.

31

Despite his aggression in Europe, Adolf Hitler (opposite) was initially very popular among the German people. Since the end of World War I in 1918, Germany had been suffering under severe economic hardship. Hitler helped Germans by creating jobs and building such new improvements as the autobahn superhighway, for which he received great political support.

taking over other nations, and he seemed ready to threaten Jews in those countries, too. Still, opposition to involvement in the war remained strong.

To strike a compromise, Roosevelt told the nation that he would not send Americans to fight overseas. Instead, America would send the Allies (Great Britain, France, and other nations) enough military supplies to enable them to defeat the Axis Powers (Germany, Italy, and Japan). Though technically neutral, the United States had chosen sides. And in September 1940, Roosevelt signed the Selective Training and Service Act. This law paved the way to draft men between the ages of twenty-one and thirty-five into the military.

The Road to War

In his State of the Union address on January 6, 1941, Roosevelt spelled out the "four essential freedoms" for which the Allies were fighting: "freedom of speech, freedom of worship, freedom from want, and freedom from fear."

In early 1941, American and British war planners held secret discussions to coordinate a military strategy against the Axis Powers. In March 1941, Congress passed the Lend-Lease Act. This law made $7 billion in aid available for Great Britain. In September, after an American ship was attacked by a German submarine, Roosevelt ordered American ships to be armed.

In October, several skirmishes occurred between American and German ships. After an American destroyer was torpedoed near Greenland, Roosevelt said, "America has been attacked, the shooting has started." On October 30, the Germans sank the U.S.S. *Reuben James*.

More than one hundred American seamen were killed in the attack. But Americans were still not ready to go to war.

Meanwhile, on the other side of the world, the Japanese were planning a surprise attack on Pearl Harbor in Hawaii. This would prove to be the event that would bring America into the war. The Japanese considered American and British economic involvement and military presence in Asia a threat to their own dominance of the region. When differences could not be settled through diplomacy, Japan prepared to attack.

On December 7, Japan carried out its attack on Pearl Harbor. Eight battleships and thirteen other naval vessels were sunk or damaged, 188 aircraft were destroyed, 2,335 United States military personnel were killed, and 1,178 were wounded. The humiliating attack finally changed Americans' minds about entering the war. Within days, America had declared war on Japan, Germany, and Italy.

Despite American concerns about the possibility of a Japanese attack, the United States naval base at Pearl Harbor was taken by complete surprise on December 7, 1941 (below). The Japanese attack nearly crippled the United States Pacific fleet, which hurt American war efforts in the early years of United States involvement.

War Against Civilians

As the war went on, it became clear that this war differed from previous wars in one important way. In many respects, World War II was a war against civilians. The Nazis in Germany eagerly helped Hitler carry out his genocidal war against the Jews. In what has come to be called the Holocaust, Hitler succeeded in murdering 6 million Jews, half of the world's total. Almost 6 million others, including Gypsies and Russian prisoners of war, were also murdered in concentration camps set up by the Nazis to eliminate those they considered inferior. Hitler also bombed cities in Great Britain and other places in Europe. During the German Army's nine-hundred-day siege of Leningrad (now St. Petersburg) in the Soviet Union, more than one third of the population of 3 million died of starvation. The German Nazis were not alone in their attacks on civilians. Seeking to force the total surrender of the Japanese military, the United States dropped atomic bombs on the cities of Hiroshima and Nagasaki. These weapons were more devastating than anything the world had seen before.

During the Holocaust, the Nazis murdered millions of their victims in gas chambers and then burned the bodies in ovens. Above, the bones of anti-Nazi German women are still in the ovens in which their bodies were burned at a concentration camp in Weimar, Germany.

American Concentration Camps

Ironically, while struggling to defeat the perpetrators of genocidal racism abroad, Americans resorted to a shameful racist policy at home. In 1942, President Roosevelt ordered the internment of more than one hundred ten thousand Japanese Americans in concentration camps, known as relocation centers, in the western deserts of the United States.

The American concentration camps were not death camps like those of the Nazis. But Japanese Americans were forced to give up their homes for the duration of the war.

After the attack on Pearl Harbor, anger at Japan quickly became directed at Japanese Americans, most of whom lived in California. On the grounds that some Japanese Americans might commit acts of sabotage, Roosevelt signed Executive Order 9066.

The fear of Japanese aggression led the United States to commit one of the most unjust acts in its history during World War II. People of Japanese heritage, regardless of citizenship, were herded into internment camps (right), where they were held in terrible conditions for the duration of the war. It was a sad time for the nation, which had traditionally prided itself on the protection of civil rights.

It provided for the roundup and evacuation of Japanese Americans to relocation centers. Families were forced to sell property in a hurry, often practically having to give it away.

When the war ended, Japanese Americans returned home to find that there was no way to get back their property. As a result of their internment in relocation centers, Japanese Americans lost more than $400 million in property and income.

Even though they had been subjected to terrible treatment, most Japanese Americans remained loyal to the United States. Many were determined to show their loyalty by making American flags and saluting them each morning. Young Japanese-American men even served in the armed forces. One regiment was made up of camp internees, the other of Japanese soldiers from Hawaii. The all-Japanese 442nd Regimental Combat Team became one of the most highly honored military units in American history.

Fighting for Civil Rights

Japanese Americans were not the only minority in the United States during the 1940s who were the victims of racism. African Americans had long been struggling against discrimination, and the 1940s brought some progress.

In January 1941, A. Philip Randolph, the head of the Brotherhood of Sleeping Car Porters, an all-black union, organized the March on Washington Movement (MOWM). The MOWM made plans for a huge march

During the years before and during World War II, huge numbers of African Americans moved from the South to the North and West to work in wartime factories. This so-called Great Black Migration continued through the 1940s. This mass movement of people had a big effect on American society as African-American sections of cities arose. Because of racism, African Americans were often paid much less than their white counterparts. As a result, black sections of cities (above) were often poor and crime-ridden.

Especially in the South, African Americans still faced terrible discrimination in the 1940s. The most humiliating form of discrimination was the Jim Crow system, which created separate public facilities, such as waiting rooms (above), for blacks and whites.

on Washington by African Americans. The marchers would demand an end to discrimination in defense plants and segregation in the armed forces. When President Roosevelt learned of this march, he issued Executive Order 8802. It called for an end to discrimination in government agencies, job-training programs, and by defense contractors. Randolph called off the march. Segregation continued in the military until July 1948, when President Truman ended it with an executive order.

One of the most influential labor and civil rights leaders in American history, Randolph also set up the Fair Employment Practices Committee to oversee the way Roosevelt's Executive Order 8802 was carried out.

Although millions of African Americans served in the military overseas, the armed forces were segregated throughout the war. All-black combat units served with distinction under General George Patton at the Battle of the Bulge during the winter of 1944–1945. Even so, African Americans, having risked their lives fighting for their country, still had a long fight ahead to win full civil rights.

The War in Europe

The war in Europe had started on September 1, 1939, when Hitler invaded Poland. Great Britain and France had responded by declaring war on Germany. But things did not go well for the British and French armies.

In the spring of 1940, Hitler trapped the British Army in France between his forces and the sea. Between May 27 and June 4, about 340,000 British soldiers were

German soldiers occupied France in June 1940. Below, a Frenchman is seen weeping as he watches the Germans enter Paris. After the Germans occupied France, a government was set up under Henri Philippe Pétain. Known as Vichy France, Pétain's government supported the Nazis.

Hitler's Nazi troops invaded the Soviet Union (above) in June 1941. The attack turned out to be a mistake. By January 1943, the brutal winter conditions in Russia, combined with the fierce counterattack offered by Russian soldiers, led to the first major German defeat of World War II.

Benito Mussolini (opposite, at left) was the fascist dictator of Italy. He allied his nation with Hitler's Nazi Germany in World War II, hoping to conquer new territory and create an Italian empire in Europe.

evacuated from the beaches at Dunkirk in hundreds of small boats.

On June 17, 1940, Hitler's army occupied Paris and set up a puppet government, with Vichy as its capital. Next on Hitler's agenda was an invasion of England. This proved to be a mistake. All of Hitler's air power and bombs failed to force the British to give up. So Hitler turned to a new target, in the east: the Soviet Union. This, too, would prove to be a mistake.

In 1939, Joseph Stalin, the leader of the Soviet Union, had shocked the world by signing a nonaggression pact with Hitler. The two dictators agreed not to attack each other and to divide Eastern Europe between themselves.

On June 22, 1941, however, Hitler launched a massive surprise invasion of the Soviet Union. More than 3 million men attacked. Facing only light resistance from the Soviet Army, which was not prepared for Hitler's *blitzkrieg*, or "lightning war," the Nazi invaders quickly captured much of the Ukraine in the western Soviet Union.

The German Army came close to Moscow but was unable to advance any farther. The Germans were also unable to capture Leningrad, even after a nine-hundred-day siege. But it was at Stalingrad that the Nazis suffered their greatest defeat.

On January 31, 1943, after five months of brutal fighting, the Germans surrendered to the Soviets. Stalingrad had been totally destroyed. Seven hundred fifty thousand Russian soldiers and civilians were dead. But the Germans had lost about two hundred thousand men, and another one hundred eight thousand were taken prisoner. This was the first major Nazi defeat of the war. It was also the beginning of the end for Hitler.

American President Franklin Roosevelt and British Prime Minister Winston Churchill had worked out a strategy for winning the war. They would enter an alliance with Stalin, even though neither trusted the Soviet dictator. Stalin, on the other hand, suspected that his new allies were only too happy to let Russia bear the worst of the Nazi aggression. In fact, the Soviet

The Holocaust was perhaps the worst genocidal event in human history. Above, in a scene at a German death camp, the grizzly evidence of Nazi racial hatred can be seen. Sadly, the bodies shown are less than half those actually discovered at the camp pictured.

Union suffered far greater losses than any other nation. By the time the war was over, 25 million Soviets had died, compared with 2 million British and 322,000 Americans.

After Stalingrad, the Soviet Army began its push westward, retaking the lands occupied by the Nazis. In July 1943, the Soviets defeated the Germans at Kursk. Meanwhile, the Allies, having defeated the German and Italian forces in North Africa, invaded Sicily on July 10, 1943. They were now prepared to invade mainland Italy. On July 25, Italian dictator Benito Mussolini was forced to resign. Italy surrendered to the Allies on September 3, 1943.

Meanwhile, Hitler grew obsessed with carrying out his "Final Solution" to the so-called "Jewish problem." In the spring of 1943, while his armies were being destroyed by the Soviets, Hitler seemed more intent on murdering the last of the Jews in the Warsaw ghetto. Most of the half million Jews who had been confined to the Warsaw ghetto in 1940 had already been sent to concentration camps. Knowing that they were doomed, the Jews still in the ghetto mounted an armed uprising against the Nazis in April 1943. Weeks later, in May, the battle was over. The Nazi troops had totally destroyed the ghetto, killing most of the defenders. Only a handful of Jewish fighters managed to escape by way of the Warsaw sewers.

However, the Nazis were losing the war. Roosevelt, Churchill, and Stalin met in Teheran, Iran, in November and December 1943 to plan "Operation Overlord"—the D-Day invasion of France, which was still occupied by the Germans.

The D-Day invasion, under the command of General Dwight D. Eisenhower, took place on June 6, 1944. Five

The Big Three, as the leaders of the Allied nations were often called, met in November 1943 at Teheran to discuss plans for the Allied invasion of occupied France. Below, left to right, are Soviet leader Joseph Stalin, United States President Franklin Roosevelt, and British Prime Minister Winston Churchill.

General Dwight David Eisenhower (above, at right) commanded the successful D-Day invasion of France. He would later win great success as a Republican politician. A war hero to American people, he served as United States president from 1953 to 1961.

In what has become perhaps the most famous invasion of World War II, Allied troops stormed the coast of France on June 6, 1944 (above). The attack would drive the Germans out of France, freeing the nation from Nazi occupation.

thousand ships carried 156,000 men across the English Channel in the largest seaborne invasion in history. When the Allied forces came ashore, they suffered heavy casualties before securing the beaches at Normandy, France. On August 25, United States troops, along with French troops under General Charles de Gaulle, entered Paris and freed the city from German rule.

In February 1945, at the Yalta Conference, Roosevelt, Churchill, and Stalin worked out plans for the postwar occupation of Germany. Soviet troops entered Berlin, Germany, in mid-April and fought a final victorious battle against Nazi troops. Germany surrendered to the Allies on May 8. Known as V-E ("Victory in Europe") day, it marked the end of World War II in Europe.

Roosevelt, who was serving his fourth term in office as president, never lived to see the victory. He died of a stroke on April 12, 1945. His vice president, Harry Truman, took over the presidency.

The Axis leaders, too, suffered death as the war came to a close. Benito Mussolini was murdered on April 28 by Italian partisans. And Adolf Hitler and his wife, Eva

Braun, committed suicide on April 30, during the last days of the Battle of Berlin.

The War in the Pacific

While war raged in Europe, Japanese forces were on the march throughout Southeast Asia and the Pacific. By July 1942, the Japanese occupied islands in the Pacific, Manchuria, eastern China, Korea, Burma, Thailand, Singapore, French Indochina, Malaya, New Guinea, and the Philippines.

The United States had suffered a humiliating blow at Pearl Harbor. But American morale began to improve when the United States Navy defeated the Japanese at the Battle of the Coral Sea in May 1942. Then on June 4–6, United States Navy pilots under the command of

In March 1942, the Japanese had taken control of the Philippine Islands, forcing American forces to flee. At that time, General Douglas MacArthur vowed, "I shall return!" And return he did. MacArthur (below, at center) waded ashore during the Allied landing at Leyte Gulf.

In one of the most memorable images of World War II (above), taken by photographer Joe Rosenthal, United States soldiers raise the American flag on Iwo Jima in February 1945.

The news of Japan's surrender sent American cities into wild excitement and relief. A New York neighborhood (opposite) is seen during its celebration of the end of the war.

Admiral Chester Nimitz succeeded in destroying Japan's main naval force during the Battle of Midway.

One by one, the Pacific Islands were won from the Japanese. America won major victories at Guadalcanal in the Solomon Islands, the Bismarck Sea, the Gilbert Islands, the Marshall Islands, and the Philippine Sea.

American General Douglas MacArthur recaptured the Philippines in October 1944. During the Battle of Leyte Gulf, the Japanese resorted to suicidal "kamikaze" attacks, crashing their planes into American ships.

In November, American pilots began a series of bombing raids on Japan. Further American victories occurred during the first half of 1945 at Iwo Jima and Okinawa. In May 1945, the Allies retook Burma.

On August 6, after Japan refused to surrender, President Truman ordered the dropping of an atomic bomb on Hiroshima. On August 9, an atomic bomb was also dropped on Nagasaki. On August 14, Japan surrendered to the Allies.

As Supreme Allied Commander, General Douglas MacArthur (above, at table) signed the Japanese surrender agreement in September 1945, then took control of rebuilding the devastated nation of Japan and helping the country start a new, democratic form of government.

Picking Up the Pieces

When the fighting ended and the celebrations were over, it was time to put together a world that had been smashed to bits. Survivors stumbled through destroyed cities, searching for food. Fortunately for Americans, the United States had been spared the ravages of war. So America was faced with the task of leading the recovery and rebuilding of the ruined nations, including the defeated enemies—Germany, Italy, and Japan.

First, there was the matter of bringing to justice those who were guilty of war crimes. The Allies held trials in Nuremberg, Germany. All the Nazi leaders brought to trial claimed they were not guilty—they were just obeying orders. This so-called "Nuremberg defense" was ignored. Some Nazis were hanged. Others received lengthy prison terms.

In Japan, former Premier Hideki Tojo and six others were indicted on fifty-five counts of war crimes. The seven were condemned to hang. Tojo was executed on December 23, 1948.

The Marshall Plan

In June 1947, George C. Marshall, the United States secretary of state, proposed a massive economic aid package for Europe to alleviate "hunger, poverty, desperation, and chaos." The American government hoped the Marshall Plan would encourage Western European countries to install or keep democratic governments rather than becoming Communist. At the same time, the United States hoped to create a market for American goods.

The Postwar World and the Start of the Cold War

Also in 1947, President Truman announced a strategy for containing communism. The plan would try to prevent communism from spreading beyond those nations where it already existed. This led to increasing friction with the Soviet Union. In April 1949, the United States and its European allies created the North Atlantic Treaty Organization (NATO), a mutual defense alliance to protect members against Soviet attack.

After the war, Germany was divided into four zones: British, French, Soviet, and American. The Soviets occupied the eastern zone. The city of Berlin was divided into French, American, British, and Soviet sectors. As relations between America and the Soviet Union deteriorated, West Berlin became a flashpoint. Because West Berlin lay within the eastern zone of Germany, the Soviets controlled access to the city. When relations became especially tense in 1948, the Soviets blocked all traffic from reaching West Berlin from the west. So America and Great Britain mounted an airlift of supplies to West Berlin that lasted from June 1948 until May 1949. On May 23, 1949, during the Berlin Airlift, the

British, French, and American occupation zones of Germany became the Federal Republic of Germany (West Germany). Civilian rule began there in September 1949. On October 7, 1949, the Soviet zone became the German Democratic Republic (Communist East Germany). The other countries of Eastern Europe, one by one, through the postwar years, became Communist satellites of the Soviet Union. An "Iron Curtain," in the words of Winston Churchill, descended across Europe, dividing the Communist East from the democratic West.

In Japan, meanwhile, American occupation forces under the command of General Douglas MacArthur began the process of transforming that nation into a democracy. Although Emperor Hirohito was allowed to keep his title, his role would be solely ceremonial.

Hopes for a Peaceful World

Once before, there had been an attempt to preserve peace in the world. After World War I, the Treaty of Versailles had provided for the establishment of a League of Nations. Unfortunately, an isolationist America had refused to join the League, and it ultimately failed to keep the peace. In 1945, there could be no turning away from the goal of peace among nations. In June 1945, fifty nations, including the United States and the Soviet Union, signed the United Nations Charter. The charter pledged "to save succeeding generations from the scourge of war." The new peacekeeping organization consisted of several parts, including the General Assembly, in which each member nation could cast its vote, and the Security Council, which has eleven members. The Security Council has six rotating members and five permanent ones: the United States, the Soviet Union (now Russia), Great Britain, France, and China. Each permanent member can veto any Security Council action.

In 1946, President Truman appointed Eleanor Roosevelt, widow of the late president, as a delegate to the United Nations (UN). On December 10, 1948, the UN Commission on Human Rights approved the Universal Declaration of Human Rights, which Eleanor Roosevelt had helped write. For many years, she had worked to promote human rights and justice in the world. In the years to come, Eleanor Roosevelt would continue to be an inspiration to American women, working to make the world a better place.

Eleanor Roosevelt (above), wife of the late President Franklin Roosevelt, was one of the most outspoken and active First Ladies of all time. After her husband's death, she continued to support charities and work for social justice in the United States and around the world. Her efforts won her an appointment as a delegate to the United Nations.

Great Britain and the Independence of India

New challenges to a peaceful world seemed to be popping up all over. Great Britain, realizing it could no longer maintain its global empire, granted independence to its

Gandhi is seen above at left with Lord Mountbatten, the last British viceroy of India, in 1946. Through Gandhi's peaceful efforts of resistance, India finally won its independence from Great Britain in 1948.

colony India. On August 15, 1947, British official Lord Louis Mountbatten, the last viceroy (British ruler) of India, partitioned India into two independent countries— India and Pakistan—because of what seemed to be irreconcilable differences between Hindus and Muslims. Almost immediately, fighting broke out. The tensions also led to the death of Mohandas "Mahatma" Gandhi, the man who had led the resistance to British rule and had inspired people all over the world with his ideals of nonviolence. On January 30, 1948, Gandhi was assassinated by a Hindu fanatic who was angry at Gandhi's efforts to bring about equal treatment for all Indians, regardless of their religion.

The Creation of Israel

Much of the Middle East, including Palestine, had also been under the control of Great Britain. Palestine's population of Arabs greatly outnumbered its Jewish population. Palestine had once been the homeland of the Jewish people. Although the Romans had driven most of Palestine's Jews into exile eighteen hundred years earlier, a small population of Jews had always lived there. Their numbers began to increase as Jewish refugees from the Holocaust in Europe arrived. After the war, survivors of the Holocaust also came. Fighting often broke out between Jews and Arabs.

In 1947, the British gave up control of Palestine to the United Nations. The General Assembly decided to separate Palestine into a Jewish section and an Arab section. The Arabs did not accept this plan. When the Jews announced the birth of their new nation of Israel on May 14, 1948, within hours, Arab armies from Egypt, Syria, Iraq, Jordan, and Lebanon attacked. Israel won its desperate struggle for survival, but seeds of bitterness were sown that would lead to more wars in the future.

After the Holocaust, many European Jews wanted to leave Europe to settle in a new place, hoping to escape the area where so many millions had been murdered. In 1948, Israel was created as a homeland for the Jews. These young Jewish women (below) are on their way to Palestine, which would become Israel, after their release from the concentration camp at Buchenwald.

The Chinese Civil War

China in the late 1940s was the scene of a brutal civil war between Mao Zedong's Communists and Jiang Jieshi's Nationalists. The civil war had actually begun in the 1930s, but it was suspended when Japan invaded China in 1937. Both sides then united to resist the Japanese. Once Japan surrendered in 1945, the civil war resumed. Ultimately, Mao's forces prevailed. Jiang and his supporters fled to the island of Taiwan. There, they remained, claiming to be the legitimate Chinese government. By October 1949, Mao had gained control of all of mainland China. He proclaimed it the People's Republic of China. Now American policy makers were faced with a huge new Communist nation and the threat of a potential new enemy.

Wonder Drugs

The antibiotic known as penicillin had been discovered accidentally on mold in 1928. In 1941, it was first used successfully to treat a bacterial infection. The timing of this medical development could not have been better. American army medics would soon be faced with huge numbers of wounded soldiers in need of something to stop infection. Luckily, they now had penicillin, which went into mass production in 1943. After testing several kinds of mold, scientists discovered streptomycin in 1944. In 1945, it became the first antibiotic used successfully in the treatment of tuberculosis.

The army had another reason to be grateful to scientists. United States troops fighting in the jungles of the South Pacific frequently came down with malaria, a deadly tropical illness transmitted by mosquitoes. In 1944, when scientists achieved the first total synthesis of quinine, they discovered that their quinine derivatives were more effective in fighting malaria than natural quinine. Soon, this new type of quinine was on its way to fight malaria in the Pacific.

The First Computer

World War II was not the only event of the 1940s that would change the world. In 1946, the University of Pennsylvania created the first computer. Called ENIAC (Electronic Numerical Integrator and Computer), it could perform the functions of an ordinary calculator,

Thanks to an accidental discovery in the 1920s, scientists were eventually able to use penicillin, which is found in certain kinds of mold, to treat many bacterial illnesses through injections (above).

The first computer, ENIAC (opposite), is seen with one of its designers, J. Presper Eckert, Jr. Because of its huge size and cost, ENIAC was not a practical machine for the public's use. However, it was a big step on the road to the development of the personal computers Americans use every day.

but it could do so a thousand times faster than ever before. Using the flow of electrons over vacuum tubes, ENIAC was a breakthrough in science and technology. When the United States War Department made use of the computer in February 1946, it was the first organization to make the leap into what would eventually become the computer age.

The Instant Camera

Perhaps not as world-changing as the first computer, another invention of the 1940s would make photography a lot more fun for many Americans. In 1948, Edwin Herbert Land introduced the Polaroid Land Camera. The camera was different because it could, in a sense, be its own darkroom—developing film within about sixty seconds. The new Polaroid was a huge success throughout the United States.

The atomic bomb dropped on Hiroshima (below) caused far more damage than any weapon ever designed up to that time. The development of nuclear weapons would change the world, as nations raced to create stronger and more deadly weapons through the Cold War years.

The Manhattan Project

The most important scientific and technological breakthrough of the 1940s, for better or worse, was the creation of the atomic bomb. Scientists were racing against time to harness the power of the atom into a weapon of mass destruction. Three physicists—Albert Einstein, who had fled to America from Nazi Germany; Enrico Fermi, who had fled to America from Italy; and Leo Szilard, who had sought refuge in London—had written to President Franklin Roosevelt, urging that the United States government try to develop nuclear weapons. It seemed certain that Adolf Hitler's scientists were attempting to do this, and it was imperative that the Allies win this race.

The Manhattan Project, which began in 1942, was the largest project in the history of science. It was directed by General Leslie Groves of the Army Corps of Engineers. Total secrecy was imposed. Key people in the project were given code names. For example, Enrico Fermi was called "Henry Farmer." Eventually, thirty-seven separate facilities employed as many as forty-three thousand people, all of them engaged in research leading to the building of the atomic bomb. However, there was so much secrecy that many of the researchers did not even know the goal of the project.

J. Robert Oppenheimer was in charge of the research complex at Los Alamos, New Mexico. It was there that the atomic bomb was built and tested. On July 16, 1945, the bomb was mounted on a steel tower and detonated. When Oppenheimer saw the giant fireball of the nuclear explosion and the mushroom cloud that rose forty thousand feet into the sky, he knew that the project had been successful. But he also wondered what horrifying implications this scientific achievement would hold for the world. "I am become death, the shatterer of worlds," were the words from a Hindu religious text that Oppenheimer recalled at that moment.

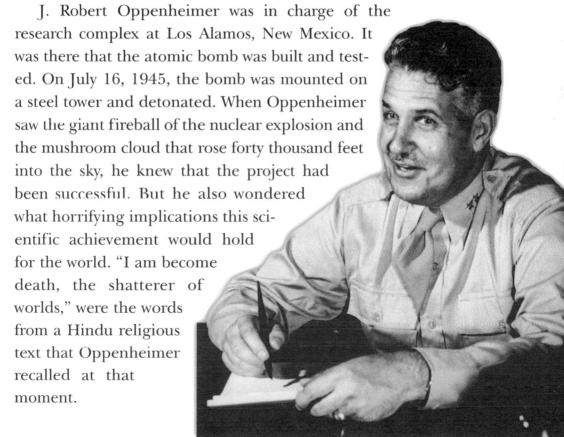

Leslie Groves (below), who was also in charge of building the Department of Defense's Pentagon building, took charge of the Manhattan Project in September 1942. He was responsible not only for the success of the project, but for selecting the sites where the bomb would be built and tested and hiring the people who would work on the atomic bomb.

For your country's sake today—

For your own sake tomorrow

GO TO THE NEAREST RECRUITING STATION
OF THE ARMED SERVICE OF YOUR CHOICE

An Amazing Decade

World War II was the defining event of the decade of the 1940s, and perhaps of the twentieth century. It was truly worldwide in scope, affecting people in every corner of the globe. The postwar world would be a very different place from the world that existed before the war. In coming decades, the nuclear weapons that were a product of World War II would serve as a deterrent, ultimately preventing both sides in the coming Cold War from launching an all-out "hot" war.

But the 1940s saw more than just war. In response to the tensions in Europe, Americans looked for new ways to have fun. Hollywood produced classic films, people danced to the wild moves of the jitterbug, and singer Frank Sinatra captured the hearts of teenage girls all over the country. It was a decade of remarkable contrast and innovation.

World War II drastically changed the face of the world and United States society. As seen in this poster (opposite), the war profoundly changed the lives of American women, who left the domestic sphere for the first time to become important members of the working world and even the military.

World War II was the greatest man-made catastrophe in human history. The immense, widespread destruction and the staggering loss of life—civilian as well as military—almost defy the imagination. Among the 55 million people who died were those killed in the Holocaust and by the atomic bomb (left).

59

1940—German Army occupies Paris, France; Germans carry out *blitz* bombing of London; Du Pont introduces nylon; Anti-Nazi films *The Great Dictator* (starring Charlie Chaplin, left) and *I Married a Nazi* are released in theaters; Richard Wright's *Native Son* is published; In September, President Franklin Roosevelt signs the Selective Training and Service Act; Roosevelt wins a third term as president in November.

1941—On January 6, Roosevelt (left) gives his State of the Union address; Also in January, A. Philip Randolph organizes the March on Washington Movement to fight for an end to racial discrimination; In March, Congress passes the Lend-Lease Act, which will indirectly assist the Allied war effort; In June, Hitler invades the Soviet Union; On October 30, Germans sink the U.S.S. *Reuben James*; On December 7, Japan bombs Pearl Harbor; The United States enters World War II; Office of Price Administration begins rationing supplies in late December; *The Maltese Falcon* (starring Humphrey Bogart, below left) is released; Penicillin is first used to treat bacterial infection.

1942—The United States Navy defeats the Japanese at the Battle of the Coral Sea; United States destroys Japan's main naval force at the Battle of Midway; In June, the Office of War Information is created; President Roosevelt orders the internment of more than one hundred thousand Japanese Americans; *Casablanca* is released; The Manhattan Project begins.

1943—On January 31, the Germans surrender to the Soviets at Stalingrad; In June, the Zoot Suit Riot takes places in Los Angeles; On July 25, Italian dictator Benito Mussolini resigns; Italy surrenders to Allies on September 3; *The North Star* is released; Orson Welles's *Citizen Kane* is released; *Oklahoma!* premieres; All-American Girls Professional Baseball League begins.

1944—Allies' D-Day invasion of France takes place on June 6; Bobby-soxers riot outside Frank Sinatra's concert in New York City in October; American General Douglas MacArthur (left) recaptures the Philippine Islands from Japan.

1945—Yalta Conference takes place in February; Roosevelt dies on April 12; Mussolini is murdered on April 28; Hitler (right) commits suicide on April 30; Germany surrenders to the Allies in May; Allies retake Burma; In June, fifty nations sign the United Nations Charter; On July 16, the first atomic bomb is tested; On August 6 and 9, the United States drops atomic bombs (right, second from top) on Hiroshima and Nagasaki, Japan; V-J day takes place on August 15; Richard Wright's *Black Boy* is published; *Carousel* premieres.

1946—The bikini bathing suit, named for the Pacific island Bikini Atoll, is introduced; Broadway musical *Annie Get Your Gun* premieres; University of Pennsylvania introduces the first computer, ENIAC.

1947—House Committee on Un-American Activities (HUAC) is established; In June, George Marshall unveils the Marshall Plan to rebuild Europe; In August, Great Britain partitions India, granting the former colony independence; In October, HUAC holds the "Hollywood Ten" hearings; Tennessee Williams's *A Streetcar Named Desire* is introduced; Jackie Robinson becomes the first African-American major-league baseball player.

1948—On January 30, Mohandas Gandhi (right) is assassinated; Norman Mailer's *The Naked and the Dead* is published; *Kiss Me, Kate* premieres; First Olympic Games since 1936 take place; On May 14, the new nation of Israel is established; In June, Berlin Airlift begins; In July, jockey Eddie Arcaro and racehorse Citation win the Triple Crown; On December 10, the United Nations approves the Universal Declaration of Human Rights; Edwin Herbert Land introduces the Polaroid Land Camera.

1949—Arthur Miller's *Death of a Salesman* is introduced; Jackie Robinson (right) is named the National League's Most Valuable Player; On May 23, West Germany becomes the Federal Republic of Germany; On October 7, East Germany becomes the German Democratic Republic; Mao Zedong establishes the Communist People's Republic of China.

Books

Evans, Harold. *The American Century*. New York: Alfred A. Knopf, 1998.

Gonzales, Doreen. *The Manhattan Project and the Atomic Bomb in American History*. Berkeley Heights, N.J.: Enslow Publishers, Inc., 2000.

Jennings, Peter, and Todd Brewster. *The Century*. New York: Doubleday, 1998.

Junior Chronicle of the 20th Century. New York: DK Publishing, 1997.

Internet Addresses

The Avalon Project. "The Avalon Project: The Atomic Bombings of Hiroshima and Nagasaki." *The Avalon Project at the Yale Law School*. 1998. <http://www.yale.edu/lawweb/avalon/abomb/mpmenu.htm>.

The Holocaust History Project. April 16, 2000. <http://www.holocaust-history.org/>.

The National D-Day Museum. n.d. <http://www.ddaymuseum.org/home.htm>.

Pearl Harbor: Remembered. March 19, 2000. <http://www.execpc.com/~dschaaf/mainmenu.html>.

ThinkQuest. *World War II: The Homefront*. 1998. <http://library.thinkquest.org/15511/>.

White House Historical Association. "Franklin D. Roosevelt." *The Presidents*. <http://www.whitehouse.gov/history/presidents/fr32.html>.

———. "Harry S Truman." *The Presidents*. n.d. <http://www.whitehouse.gov/history/presidents/ht33.html>.